The Well-Versed

BIBLE VERSE JOURNAL

featuring 30 full-color illustrated verses on

Hope and Encouragement

Read & Journal a Bible Verse Each Day For 30 Days

copyright © 2018 The Well Versed Day
Find The Way Publishing
All Rights Reserved

No part of this publication may be reproduced, distributed, or transmitted in any form or by any means, including photocopying, recording, or any other electronic or mechanical methods, without the prior written permission of the publisher.

May the *God* of hope fill you with all *joy* and *peace* as you trust in him, so that you may overflow with *hope* by the power of the Holy Spirit.

Romans 15:13

Date: _____

This verse in my life right now:
_____
_____
_____
_____
_____
_____
_____
_____
_____
_____
_____
_____
_____
_____
_____

I am praying about:
_____
_____
_____
_____

I am grateful for:
_____
_____
_____
_____

For I know the *plans* I have for you, declares the *Lord*, plans to *prosper* you and not to harm you, plans to give you *hope* and a *future*.

Jeremiah 29:11

Date: _____

This verse in my life right now:
_____
_____
_____
_____
_____
_____
_____
_____
_____
_____
_____
_____
_____
_____
_____
_____

I am praying about:

_____
_____
_____
_____

I am grateful for:

_____
_____
_____
_____

This verse in my life right now: Date: _____

_____
_____
_____
_____
_____
_____
_____
_____
_____
_____
_____
_____
_____
_____
_____

I am praying about: **I am grateful for:**

_____   _____
_____   _____
_____   _____
_____   _____

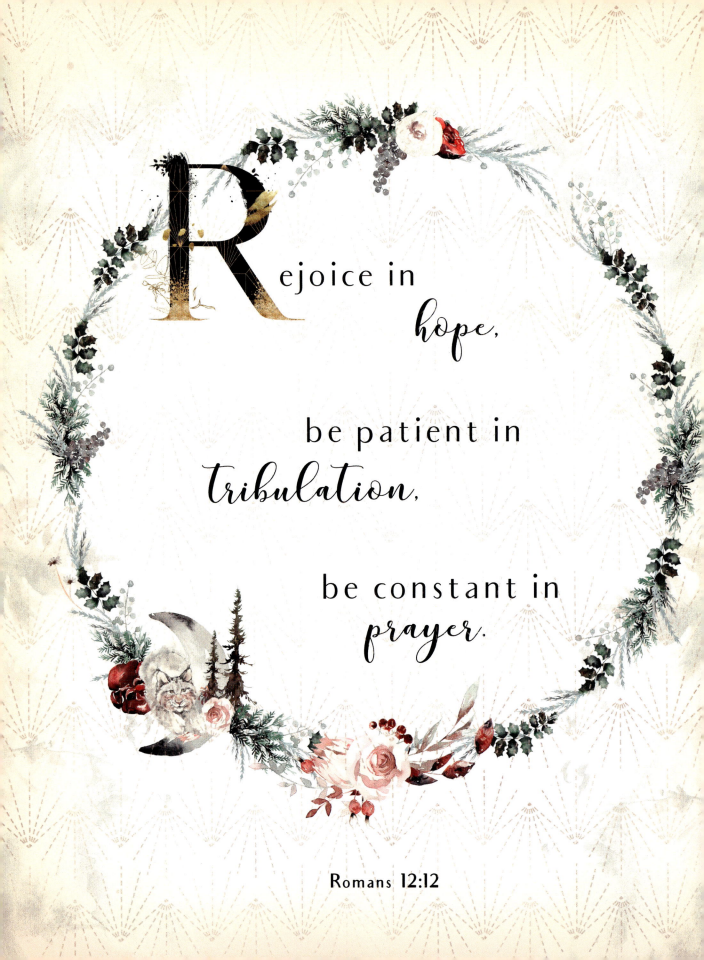

Date: _____

This verse in my life right now:
_____
_____
_____
_____
_____
_____
_____
_____
_____
_____
_____
_____
_____
_____
_____

I am praying about:

_____
_____
_____
_____

I am grateful for:

_____
_____
_____
_____

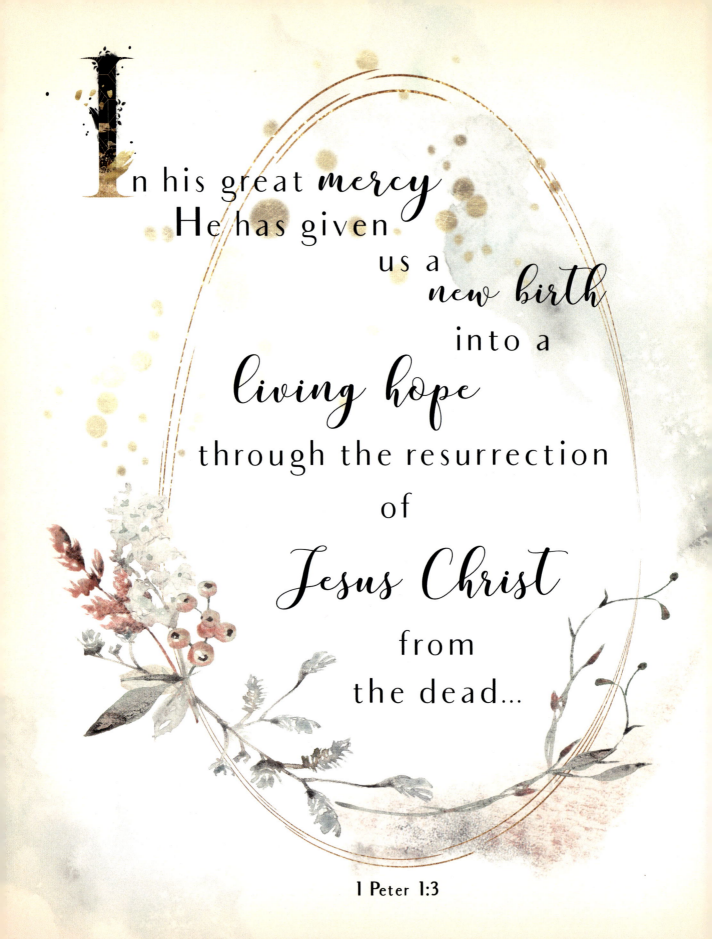

In his great *mercy* He has given us a *new birth* into a *living hope* through the resurrection of *Jesus Christ* from the dead...

1 Peter 1:3

Date: _____

This verse in my life right now:
_____
_____
_____
_____
_____
_____
_____
_____
_____
_____
_____
_____
_____
_____
_____
_____

I am praying about:
_____
_____
_____
_____

I am grateful for:
_____
_____
_____
_____

This verse in my life right now: Date: _____

I am praying about:

I am grateful for:

Date: _____

This verse in my life right now:
_____
_____
_____
_____
_____
_____
_____
_____
_____
_____
_____
_____
_____
_____
_____

I am praying about:
_____
_____
_____
_____

I am grateful for:
_____
_____
_____
_____

What no eye has *seen*, what no ear has *heard*, and what no human mind has ever *conceived* – the things *God* has prepared for those who *love* Him.

1 Corinthians 2:9

Date: _____

This verse in my life right now:
_____
_____
_____
_____
_____
_____
_____
_____
_____
_____
_____
_____
_____
_____
_____
_____
_____

I am praying about:
_____
_____
_____
_____

I am grateful for:
_____
_____
_____
_____

You have been my hope, Sovereign Lord, my confidence since my youth.

Psalm 71:5

Date: _____

This verse in my life right now:

I am praying about:

I am grateful for:

Date: _____

This verse in my life right now:
_____
_____
_____
_____
_____
_____
_____
_____
_____
_____
_____
_____
_____
_____
_____
_____
_____
_____
_____
_____

I am praying about:

_____
_____
_____
_____
_____

I am grateful for:

_____
_____
_____
_____
_____

If you have *faith* as small as a mustard seed, you can say to this *mountain*, "*Move* from here to there," and it will move. *Nothing* will be *impossible* for you.

Matthew 17:20

Date: _____

This verse in my life right now:
_____
_____
_____
_____
_____
_____
_____
_____
_____
_____
_____
_____
_____
_____
_____
_____
_____
_____

I am praying about:
_____
_____
_____
_____
_____

I am grateful for:
_____
_____
_____
_____
_____

Hope that is seen is not hope. Who hopes for what they already have? But if we hope for what we do not have, we wait for it with patience.

Romans 8:24-25

Date: _____

This verse in my life right now:
_____
_____
_____
_____
_____
_____
_____
_____
_____
_____
_____
_____
_____
_____
_____
_____

I am praying about:
_____
_____
_____
_____

I am grateful for:
_____
_____
_____
_____

This verse in my life right now: Date: _____

I am praying about:

I am grateful for:

Date: _____

This verse in my life right now:
_____
_____
_____
_____
_____
_____
_____
_____
_____
_____
_____
_____
_____
_____
_____
_____
_____

I am praying about:
_____
_____
_____
_____

I am grateful for:
_____
_____
_____
_____

Blessed is the one who *perseveres* under trial, because having stood the test, he will receive the *crown of life* that the *Lord* has promised to those who *love* Him.

James 1:12

Date: _____

This verse in my life right now:
_____
_____
_____
_____
_____
_____
_____
_____
_____
_____
_____
_____
_____
_____
_____
_____
_____
_____

I am praying about:
_____
_____
_____
_____

I am grateful for:
_____
_____
_____
_____

When I said, "My foot is slipping," your unfailing love, Lord, supported me. When anxiety was great within me, your consolation brought me joy.

Psalm 94:18-19

Date: _____

This verse in my life right now:
_____
_____
_____
_____
_____
_____
_____
_____
_____
_____
_____
_____
_____
_____
_____
_____
_____
_____

I am praying about:
_____
_____
_____
_____

I am grateful for:
_____
_____
_____
_____

ow this is what the
Lord says, He who
created you...

Fear not
for I have redeemed you;
I have summoned you by name;
You are Mine.

Isaiah 43:1

Date: _____

This verse in my life right now:
_____
_____
_____
_____
_____
_____
_____
_____
_____
_____
_____
_____
_____
_____
_____
_____
_____

I am praying about:

_____
_____
_____
_____

I am grateful for:

_____
_____
_____
_____

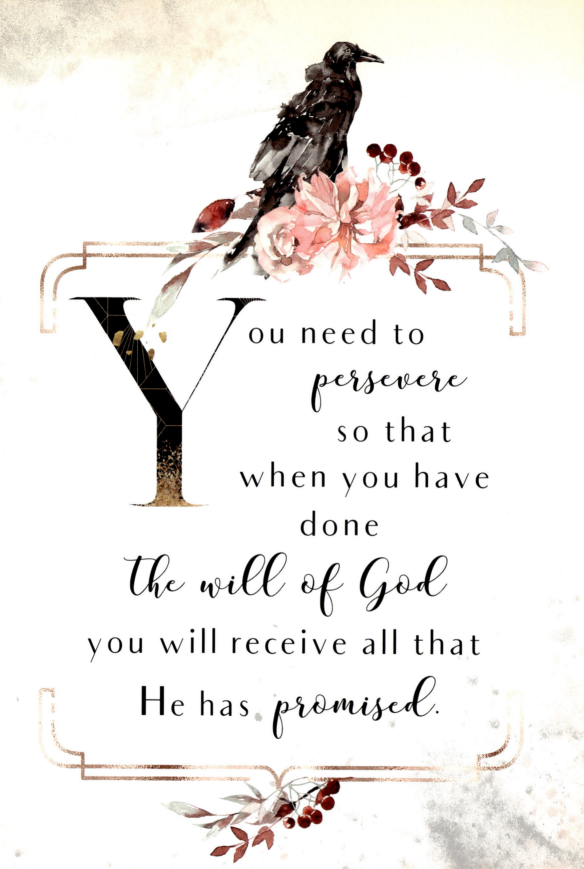

Date: _____

This verse in my life right now:
_____
_____
_____
_____
_____
_____
_____
_____
_____
_____
_____
_____
_____
_____
_____
_____
_____
_____

I am praying about:
_____
_____
_____
_____

I am grateful for:
_____
_____
_____
_____

The eyes of the Lord search the whole *earth* in order to *strengthen* those whose *hearts* are fully *committed* to Him.

2 Chronicles 16:9

This verse in my life right now: Date: _____

I am praying about:

I am grateful for:

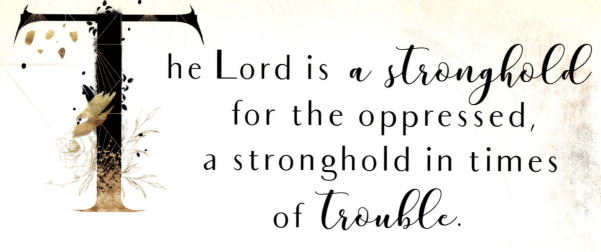

The Lord is *a stronghold* for the oppressed, a stronghold in times of *trouble*. And those who know Your name will put their trust in You, for You, *oh Lord*, have not forsaken those who *seek* You.

Psalm 9:9-10

Date: _____

This verse in my life right now:
_____
_____
_____
_____
_____
_____
_____
_____
_____
_____
_____
_____
_____
_____
_____
_____
_____
_____

I am praying about:
_____
_____
_____
_____

I am grateful for:
_____
_____
_____
_____

Now then, *stand still* and see this *great thing* the Lord is about to do before your eyes.

1 Samuel 12:16

Date: _____

This verse in my life right now:

_____
_____
_____
_____
_____
_____
_____
_____
_____
_____
_____
_____
_____
_____
_____
_____

I am praying about:

_____
_____
_____
_____

I am grateful for:

_____
_____
_____
_____

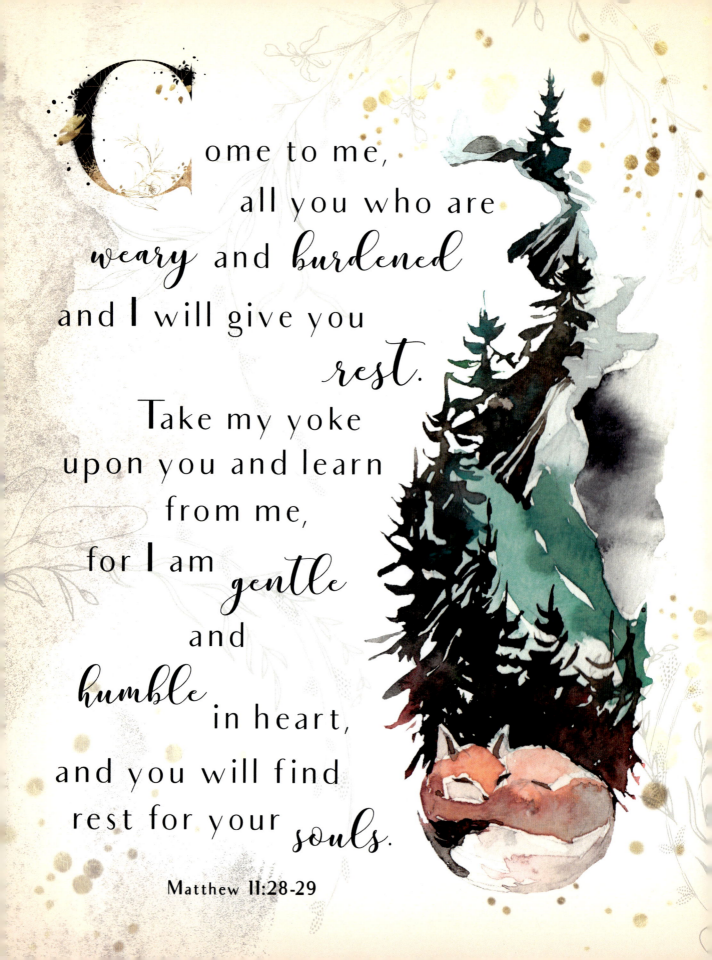

Date: _____

This verse in my life right now:
_____
_____
_____
_____
_____
_____
_____
_____
_____
_____
_____
_____
_____
_____
_____
_____
_____

I am praying about:
_____
_____
_____
_____
_____

I am grateful for:
_____
_____
_____
_____
_____

o not be *afraid* or *discouraged* because of this vast army. For the *battle* is not yours, but *God's*.

2 Chronicles 20:15

Date: _____

This verse in my life right now:

_____
_____
_____
_____
_____
_____
_____
_____
_____
_____
_____
_____
_____
_____
_____
_____

I am praying about:

_____
_____
_____
_____

I am grateful for:

_____
_____
_____
_____

And we know that in all things God works for the good of those who love Him, to them who are called according to his purpose.

Romans 8:28

Date: _____

This verse in my life right now:
_____
_____
_____
_____
_____
_____
_____
_____
_____
_____
_____
_____
_____
_____
_____
_____
_____

I am praying about:
_____
_____
_____
_____

I am grateful for:
_____
_____
_____
_____

For the sake of *Christ* I am content with weaknesses, insults, hardships, persecutions, and difficulties. For when I am weak, *then I am strong.*

2 Corinthians 12:10

Date: _____

This verse in my life right now:

I am praying about:

I am grateful for:

But those who *hope*
in the Lord
will renew their
strength.
They will
soar
on wings of eagles;
they will *run*
and not grow weary,
they will *walk*
and not
be faint.

Isaiah 40:31

Date: _____

This verse in my life right now:
_____
_____
_____
_____
_____
_____
_____
_____
_____
_____
_____
_____
_____
_____
_____

I am praying about:
_____
_____
_____
_____

I am grateful for:
_____
_____
_____
_____

For our light *affliction,*
which is only for the moment,
worketh for us
more and more
exceedingly
an eternal weight of *glory...*

2 Corinthians 4:17

Date: _____

This verse in my life right now:

I am praying about:

I am grateful for:

Date: _____

This verse in my life right now:
_____
_____
_____
_____
_____
_____
_____
_____
_____
_____
_____
_____
_____
_____
_____
_____

I am praying about:
_____
_____
_____
_____

I am grateful for:
_____
_____
_____
_____

Date: _____

This verse in my life right now:

I am praying about:

I am grateful for:

Wait for the Lord;
be strong
and take heart
and
wait for the Lord.

Psalm 27:14

Date: _____

This verse in my life right now:

I am praying about:

I am grateful for:

Download a Free
8 x 10 Printable Illustrated Verse at:
www.findthewaypublishing.com/well-versed/

Look for all of our
Well-Versed Day
Bible Verse Journals

Made in the USA
Columbia, SC
26 August 2019